When Daddy's a Drunk
— What to tell the kids

by Evelyn Leite

First Published, October 1979

Copyright©1979, by Hazelden Foundation, Inc.
All rights reserved.
No part of this book may be reproduced
without the written permission of the publisher.

ISBN: 0-89486-076-3

Printed in the United States of America

The Twelve Steps are reprinted by permission of
Alcoholics Anonymous World Services Inc.,

Printed in the United States of America

Dedicated with love and appreciation to
Lonny and Robert

Often, special problems occur in families when the father is an alcoholic. One of the main problems for the nondrinking parent is simply parenting the children — innocent bystanders who are apt to become involved in the problem as surely as are both parents. Most times, the nondrinking spouse is so busy struggling with her own feelings of confusion, anger, bitterness, and guilt and is working so hard to keep the economics of the family on an even keel that the children are lost in the disarray. Too often little attention is paid to the jumbled mix of feelings with which the children in an alcoholic family are trying to cope, jumbled feelings for which they receive scant help from any adults. Even when the nondrinking parent is aware of the children's unhappiness and frustrations, she may feel inadequate and incapable of dealing with them.

How can a parent who is facing problems from alcoholism help children face similar problems in a constructive, positive way?

The coping techniques herein are not meant to take the place of professional counseling, nor will these techniques always be effective with the more troubled child. As a parent, you must take into consideration the confusion experienced by every single member in an alcoholic family system. The special problems that will be present for children who have been physically or mentally abused can be offset if understood and dealt with, but not always at home. It is important to get help for a child who needs it; it is not an admission of failure to do so, but an indication of love and caring.

In their simplicity, children will often recognize that there is a drinking problem in the home before either parent recognizes it. Children will sometimes point this out to one or both parents only to be hushed or told to mind their own business. Children may appear calm on the outside, but inside some fears and apprehensions may be forming. Even small children can be seriously worried about the health and well-being of their parents. Children can sense trouble and unrest, and they can feel when something is wrong even when they can't see what that something is.

In some alcoholic homes the children witness enraged screaming, cold frosty silence, and petty destructive retaliations; they may witness their mother being abused or be the victim of abuse themselves. In other alcoholic homes a child may witness a drunken, lurching parent who shows kindness, generosity, joviality, and a physically harmless playfulness. Children may find themselves simply ignored by a drinking father who falls asleep every night in a chair. Children may even laugh at the drinker's antics and feel him to be grossly misunderstood by the nondrinking parent. Regardless of the kind of person the problem drinker is, sooner or later the children will suffer not only the problems so familiar to you, the nondrinking parent, but other problems perhaps not so familiar to you.

As the alcoholism goes through its steadily worsening phases, the children will become more and more confused. They will begin to feel out of kilter with the rest of the world as they experience neglect by the drinking parent. Family activities will most usually include drinking, and there will be a gradual progression in which the nondrinking parent takes on an ever greater share of the responsibilities for the family.

Children in alcoholic homes often are asked to play many different roles. They may be expected to "understand" both parents. They may be expected to be comforter and supporter to one, the other, or both. They may be asked to be perfect or to be exceptional at something they do. They may be praised one minute and clobbered the next. They may receive different sets of rules from each parent or receive conflicting directions from one moment to the next. A sense of insecurity pervades the household as the children go from day to day not knowing which role they should play at which times, or whose rules they should follow. Unwillingly these children begin to feel mistrust and anger toward both parents.

Uncertainty about what tomorrow or this day or this hour will bring will leave them fearful and bewildered. In some homes, the children may find themselves standing around waiting to see if this is the time they will be handed a dollar bill and patted on the head, or if this is one of those times when their dirty room — or the dishes — or the way they look — suddenly takes on the gigantic proportions of an abominable sin of omission. When living in a home with an alcoholic, the children discover early in life that they can seldom do the right thing at the right time.

When children are small they are especially helpless, but their helplessness does not prevent them from being witness to the process of alcoholism in their home. Uncertain, unhappy, and befuddled, they cling tighter and tighter to both the alcoholic and nonalcoholic parent on whom they are dependent. They may manifest these feelings in a myriad of ways: by making unrelenting demands, showing fear of the dark, being afraid of other people, developing nervous disorders, refusing to eat, eating too much, developing ways to get people to laugh at them, and other unbecoming behaviors. When children are older they may do all of these things plus take even more sophisticated action to express their dissatisfaction with the home situation: running away, use of drugs, and vandalism are examples.

Children learn quickly that the alcoholic is somehow incompetent and needs to be protected. More often than not children will blame the nondrinking spouse for the sad and troubled happenings in their home. Even if initially they feel that you are not to blame for the drinking parent's actions, your behavior and that of the drinker will blindly conspire to change their minds.

As the nondrinking parent, you may have denied to your children that there is a drinking problem, and thus led them to believe that excessive drinking is normal behavior. In a faulty attempt to make things easier for your children, you may have refused to discuss the drinking, or — worse — lied to them concerning the drinking. You may have tried to shield them from violence or erratic behavior by sending them to another part of the house or by sending them completely away from the home while their father was drinking. You may have watched your children be mistreated, or you may have interfered on their behalf when they were victimized. You may have behaved as if you deserved the treatment you got from the alcoholic, and thus convinced your children that you were indeed responsible for the problem drinker's behavior.

Any of the above reactions would only encourage the children to silently or openly point an accusing finger at you. As long as you react, the children may believe that you can control the drinker's behavior. They may say, "Daddy wouldn't drink so much if you would be nicer to him" or "Daddy probably would come home if you weren't so mean." And you with your burden of guilt very much intact will believe them. It is impossible for children to accept the reality of such a situation because they have been taught not to. They actually believe in their hearts that you could make Daddy behave if you really wanted to, and could stop him from hitting you, hitting them, driving that car, taking that drink, and on and on. As the children grow older and see how other children live, they will become both ashamed and protective of the drinking parent and loyal too, while at the same time being demanding of the nondrinking parent — and totally confused by the alternate feelings of love and hatred that they feel toward both parents.

Children living in an alcoholic home will learn to display symptoms similar to those of a "dry drunk." They will learn to project angry feelings onto others, while observing the controlling, over-compensating actions of the nondrinking parent. Children become adept at playing both sides of the fence, and certainly not without negative consequences for themselves. Though they may be young, the children learn how to duck trouble, manipulate and con, and they become overwhelmed with guilt for which there is no explanation. By the time you as the nondrinking parent have recognized the family problem of alcoholism, some serious behavioral problems and fundamental feelings of worthlessness have already taken root in the children.

Now that you have recognized the alcoholism, the problem is how to go about repairing some of the damage that has been done. The desire is to help your children unlearn some of their self-defeating behaviors, and to learn some ways of feeling good about themselves and coping with their lives. You may believe that the children have been protected and are unaware of trouble. It is more likely that the children are aware that something is wrong though they may not yet be aware that it is alcoholism.

Children are very much a part of the family disease of alcoholism. They are suffering, and they need to learn about alcoholism. They also need to develop some skills to deal with it as soon as possible. You may say: "But I already work my fingers to the bone to keep them in food and clothing. I do my best to protect them. I make sacrifices for them; I take care of them and most of the time they don't even appreciate it. Sometimes I think they hate me and sometimes I even think I hate them. And when I look at them I feel guilty." At this point, you may be on the verge of not only blaming your drinking spouse for all your problems but also blaming your children as well. You may feel that it is time somebody appreciated you, understood you.

In many instances, your children's seeming refusal to understand what you are going through, their seeming unappreciativeness of what you are doing for them, and their love and loyalty toward your drinking spouse are enough to make you tear out your hair in anguish and lash out at them with painful, hateful words. You may be an expert at heaping guilt on a child; you may be a "How-could-you-do-this-to-your-poor-mother" kind of parent. You may be a parent who demands that your children choose sides — your side. You may be a parent who consistently points out the other parent's faults and bad behavior, wanting the children to see things "as they really are." You may be a parent who says nothing to the children but who by silence, body movements, and facial expression conveys criticism and anger toward them and toward the drinking spouse.

You may have a quiet, docile, withdrawn child with an underdog attitude who makes you want to scream: "Do something, anything, only stop making me feel so guilty." You may have a child who excels in everything, causing you to feel mounting pride and to found all your hopes and happiness in that child. Or you may have a child who has decided the best way to avoid the trouble at home is to be in constant trouble himself.

It is vital to the well-being of the family that you drop any expectations that future sobriety will reverse all the problems that alcoholism has already caused. You — yes, you — who are already over-burdened with guilt, anger, insecurity, and overwhelming responsibility, must learn that in order to have any positive effect on your children you must be in harmony with yourself and be willing to change your own attitudes and behaviors. It is imperative that you be able to deal with the subject of alcoholism matter-of-factly and without malice or judgment. You can give up your inclinations to control your alcoholic. You can give up your self-pity and guilt. You can overcome your resentment and frustration.

There exists for most nondrinking parents a certain sense of outrage, despair and soul-searing hurt when they see their children neglected, disappointed, manipulated, punished, or lied to by the drinking parent. How can one parent offset this damage? You can begin by striving for objectivity, compassion, and self-worth. You can begin by teaching your children the same things. The only control you and your children can hope for is your own personal control over your own actions.

In Al-Anon you learn ways to control your own actions. You learn coping techniques and self-assurance. You learn about the illness of alcoholism and meet other people who are overcoming the same problems you are encountering. As you begin to recognize the scope of your own illness and the ways in which you have contributed to the family problem (e.g., silently begging their forgiveness while refusing to forgive yourself), you may find yourself trying to over-compensate with the children. Or you may be trying to ignore your own illness and still be at the point of asking: "Why me?" if your child is in constant trouble or doing poorly in school. By this time you may even have lost all loving contact with the children and feel yourself to be living in a houseful of unfriendly strangers.

In dealing with children, in addition to your recognition of the disease of alcoholism, the single most important thing is the recognition of yourself as a vital, loving, worthwhile human being. Now look at yourself — are you lovable? Are you sometimes silent, withdrawn, caught in the web of your own bitterness? Do you scream loudly for allegiance and perfection? Are you a doormat inviting everyone to walk on you? Do you slink around with a poor-little-me attitude? Do you whine for love and understanding? Do you adopt a hurt and suffering facade? Do you pretend to your children that you are the perfect parent and dare them to question it? Do you coldly control every movement in the family, even your children's leisure time and recreation?

Do you monitor your children's every move making empty threats and erratically switching from praise to put-downs, from punishment to reward? Do you demand that your children notice what you do for them and that they tell you often how good you are? Do you indicate to your children by word or gesture when they have made a mistake that they are inadequate or stupid? Do you stand guard over your children, fighting their battles, nagging them, overprotecting them, interfering in sibling arguments? Do you make dire predictions about their future? And do you as a parent expect them to THANK YOU for all this?

One method by which you can apply the teachings of the Al-Anon program to your children in a significant way is to apply the Twelve Steps in your dealings with them.

As you begin the application of these steps, keep in mind that you and your children are in no way forming an alliance against the alcoholic. You are learning survival and forming new relationships with each other. The drinking parent may see this new relationship as a threat and make attempts to thwart it, but your Al-Anon group will help you contend with this. As your strength and detachment skills develop, so will those of your children.

#1. We admitted we were powerless over alcohol, that our lives had become unmanageable. *Detach from the alcoholic*

You may have already accepted this truth for yourself, but has it *mental* ever occurred to you that your children may be feeling responsible for the drinking, and they need to be TOLD they are not?

Have you or the drinking parent blamed the children for the existing problems in the home? When you are really angry with your situation, do you sometimes catch yourself thinking that if it weren't for the children there would be less fighting, more money, more time to take care of your husband, maybe even thinking that if it weren't for them you wouldn't have to stay in this home? Admitting that you are powerless over alcoholism should allow you to see that the children have even less power than you do; that their behavior, like yours, is only a reaction to the entangling force in the home.

Admitting that you are powerless over the illness of alcoholism will also free you from having to take the whole responsibility for the problems of your children. You have the freedom to explain to your children the unmanageability and powerlessness of their lives, making sure they understand that alcoholism is an illness for which no one can be held responsible. Let them know that actions — the drinker's or someone else's — may be used as an excuse to drink but are actually irrelevant when it comes to explaining the cause of alcoholism.

When you try to explain the Al-Anon teachings to your children, you may be met with a deaf ear; if so, it is perhaps because they fear learning that alcoholism is their fault. Many times the nondrinking parent spends a lot of time trying to make the children conform to the alcoholic's inconsistent demands in an effort to avoid trouble. Or the children may think that your efforts to explain things to them are just another attack on the "poor defenseless alcoholic."

One of the better ways of beginning a new relationship with the children is to admit to them that while you cannot change anything that has happened in the past, you feel that your relationship with them could be improved in the future. Pick a quiet time to talk to your children and be sincere. Tell them that you know they are not as happy as they might be and ask them what actions OF YOURS are contributing to their pain. Your children may meet this new approach with no small amount of skepticism and you may have to assure them several times that you really want to hear what they have to say.

Keep in mind that your children have learned coping techniques and retaliatory measures that will turn you on, turn you off, and turn you upside down. Review in your mind what you have learned in Al-Anon about detachment. If in anger, your children verbally attack you, try to hear only the pain and anger underneath the words. Steel yourself not to react. A simple phrase such as: "I want very much to hear what you are saying" and a gentle question concerning their original point may interrupt a cutting attack and put the conversation back on course. Be determined to hold to an honest giving and receiving of information. Ask questions and swallow all temptation to justify your actions or to place the blame elsewhere. If you are talking to more than one child, ask that each waits a turn to talk and that close, respectful attention be paid to the one who is talking. Children who are listened to can be convinced that you really care about their feelings and ideas.

While you are hearing what each child has to say, remember that this may be the first time you as a parent have ever *just listened*. Encourage them, touch them if possible, and do your best to relieve them of any guilt they might be feeling for telling you that you are not perfect. Accept what your children are saying calmly and without hurt even though you may think many of the things they are saying are unfair. Showing signs of hurt will convince them that you only want to hear the good things about yourself. Remember, regardless of the circumstances, this is how it will seem to them.

Ask your children what one thing they feel is most important for you to change right now. Tell them you will need their understanding and patience while you concentrate on that one thing. Do not agree to change a behavior that cannot be changed — e.g., staying home more when you have to work. Do not agree to change a behavior that at this time would be overwhelming for you, because you will fail and your children may become more cynical than ever. Pick something that can actually be improved: your natural parental tendency to nag; your unconscious habit of belittling; your blackmail tactics ("If you don't behave, I won't love you").

It is imperative not to be threatened by honest criticism from your children. If you can't take it, how do you expect them to listen when you critize them? It is also imperative for you to remember that at this time you are not asking for any kind of trade off or change in their behavior; nor are you going to tell them any of their faults. Such would be blackmail and would destroy any good you are trying to accomplish. Do not bring into the discussion the alcoholic's behavior or actions; keep it strictly a "you and me" exchange.

The admission that we are "powerless" and "that our lives have become unmanageable" and beyond our control provides a sense of relief that can be conveyed to the children in an enthusiastic way. A simple statement such as: "Can you believe it? I actually thought that I could control everything that happened in this house and make things right all by myself" might clear away the last residue of pretense at control and open the door for better relationships and clearer communication.

#2. "Came to believe that a power greater than ourselves could restore us to sanity."

What is this power and how are you going to make it work for you where your children are concerned? If the power is God, have you really given in to His will or are you still expecting Him to swoop down and make things go your way? Are you so convinced that your way is the only way that you haven't given your Higher Power a chance to restore you to sanity?

A lot of people will admit to anything EXCEPT being wrong where their children are concerned. Thus, they go on making the same mistakes day after day. Many people would rather face a firing squad than admit to their children that they don't always know what is best for a particular child. Ask your Higher Power for humility that you may admit your parental imperfections. Ask Him for wisdom that you may have the ability to know when to speak up and when to shut up. Ask Him for courage to be able to look at the family objectively. Ask for guidance that you may know the right thing to do when you must act. And ask Him for the strength to demand perfection neither in self nor in others.

Take the time to talk about your children with your Higher Power. Tell Him all your fears and doubts and hopes and dreams. Give Him all your grief over past mistakes and present problems. He will accept them gladly and free your mind to deal with everyday living.

If you are now having a problem of guilt and remorse over treatment your children have received in the past, you have still not accepted your powerlessness. If you are consistently overprotective or constantly making excuses for your children's behavior, can it be related to your guilt over the past?

When children reach their early teens, they can be particularly difficult under the best of circumstances. In situations where they have a sense of guilt and worthlessness, they may try any number of things to make themselves feel better. This can be a particularly trying time for both parents and children. If your child has deliberately disobeyed you or is being impossibly difficult, you and your Higher Power can calmly and rationally deal with one problem at a time. You can resist the impulse and the luxury of lashing out in anger.

Maybe you think a particular child is very hard to manage and that he has deliberately disobeyed you. Could the word *manage* be the key to your problem? If you have been deliberately disobeyed and you are angry, you may think you should do something, only you don't know what. It would be a good idea to level with your child and tell him that you are too angry to be rational at the moment and that you need some time to think. While you are thinking, ask yourself if you are upset because your child has done something which could result in serious injury to himself or others. Or did the child's action reflect badly on you as a parent? Is your concern directed toward your child or toward what the neighbors might think? Some parents will outline a child's whole day or week leaving little room for self-expression or creativity. Other parents will say yes to anything their children want simply to avoid conflict, and they will ignore all signs of disobedience. Committing yourself and your problems to your Higher Power can help you find the middle of the road.

Whether it is a matter of grief, guilt, overanxiousness, righteous indignation, or tormenting indecision, once you have confided in your Higher Power, you will be able to decide what if any action you should take. Some guides to determining what you as a parent can do might be the following: • Ask yourself if the rules you have made are really important. • Are they for the sake of parental authority? • Are you expecting more from children than is reasonable? • Are you asking them to give you a reason to boast? • Are you perhaps asking them not to grow up so you won't have to face the growing pains that come with older children who have developed minds of their own?

Maybe you need to bone up on Al-Anon detachment techniques and learn how to let go. Even if your child has committed a serious offense, you can be loving and administer punishment in a constructive, nurturing way. Take a good look at your alternatives: most of your problems can be solved by more honesty and communication with your children. Be sure your child knows that your love never falters, even though your common sense might. Ask your Higher Power to help you to be tough when you need to be tough, soft when you need to be soft, and to help you trust Him to see you through it all.

#3 "Made a decision to turn our will and our lives over to the care of God as we understood him."

A great deal of comfort and peace can be gained when you turn your life and will over to God, and it is never too early or too late to begin teaching your children about His comfort and love. If your children are small, evening prayers, mealtime grace, and bedtime stories can instill in them a feeling of God's presence. If your children are older and your attempts to talk about God are met with scorn and disbelief, don't despair or show anxiety. If you feel uncomfortable with the subject of God, make attempts to learn as much as you can, have practice conversations with yourself or other adults, and know enough about your own beliefs to discuss them. Then quietly and calmly insert "spirituality" into your conversations occasionally. Be casual but steadfast, and let the children know that prayer is an important part of your life, if it is.

If you live and behave in such a way as to leave no doubt in your children's minds about what you believe, and if you remain calm and undeterred, most likely you will see subtle changes in their attitudes. If, as in some other homes, God and religion have always been a part of your children's lives and still they are unbelieving, perhaps it is because they are embittered because they see little of divine justice, or even, crassly, because "things have not gone their way." Maybe what you are witnessing is only the children's natural tendency to rebel. In any case, don't panic or condemn them; their best example is you.

#4 "Made a searching and fearless moral inventory of ourselves."

Step Four is a difficult Step to do because it can produce much pain and guilt. The mental anguish which can accompany the taking of this Step can be almost devastating unless you keep in mind your reason for doing it. The Step is meant to be a cleansing step, a learning process. Perhaps you have always shoved to the back of your mind the problems the children were developing as you watched and stewed while alcoholism in your home was reaping your full attention. Perhaps you have been so overwhelmed with troubles and responsibilities that you have not had the time or the strength to deal with your children's troubles.

Perhaps you have hoped that if you ignored their problems, the problems would go away. Fourth Step time is a time to examine your relationship with each child in the family and fearlessly take note of times you have caused a child needless pain, acted unreasonably, or been guilty of neglect. Fourth Step time is not the time to rehash what has been done to them by your drinking spouse or to hit yourself over the head for things that can never be changed. Stick to a list of whats; forget the whys and learn from what you see in front of you.

#5 "Admitted to God, to ourselves and to another human being the exact nature of our wrongs."

If you haven't yet taken a Fifth Step in Al-Anon, you will discover that when you do, it is purifying, refreshing, and vital to your well-being. To be able to tell a trusted, responsible person who will not judge you all your darkest, deepest shames and actions, and to discover that the person still cares about you is to find relief and hope. You will have rid yourself of a big burden that it is time to be rid of, if you are to grow in mind and spirit. Even if you have taken this Step once, I would urge you to do it again with just your children in mind. Often, we are so concerned with other wrongs that the children are only considered incidentally. Again, do not bring into your Fifth Step actions for which your alcoholic spouse may have been responsible.

In the actual writing out and telling of your interaction with your children, you will catch new insights and you may discover you did many things right. In any case, you will be able to clear your conscience, see better ways of relating to your children, and focus on your responsibilities to them.

Parents will often try to make up with their children by moaning or weeping on children's shoulders about wrongs they have done the children in the past; or parents will buy them expensive presents. To do either is patent self-indulgence and both actions burden the children with on-the-spot forgiveness for things they may not even understand. Such ill-planned behavior can only cause the children more unhappiness than they have. It is right and good to be able to admit you have made a mistake and to be able to sincerely apologize for something that has just happened. To do so only shows good manners and humanness. If your children bring up some unhappy experience from the past, you can say: "Yes, I see now that I made a mistake," or "Yes, I did behave badly in that situation." Then say no more. Your children have what they want, which is your admission that you are not infallible and your reaffirmation of their judgment of right and wrong.

#6 "Were entirely ready to have God remove all these defects of character."

Parents who are overly concerned about how they look to others will develop elaborate schemes and rules to make sure that their children reflect well on them. Some will even try to live their lives through their children. Step Six helps you decide what is really important. You can pray for God's help in letting you overlook the things that are not. Step Six urges you to ask God to help you back off and let your children establish their own priorities.

Who really cares if your kids prefer patched jeans to dress pants or dresses? Who should care if a daughter has ears pierced or wears combat boots? Whose business is it if a son's hair is long or short? Why should it matter to anyone else if your children are not interested in sports, music, or any other discipline?

If your children's grades are not up to snuff, who is going to suffer? Who? Who? Who? If your answer is some vague THEY (as in "THEY will think I am a poor parent"), you are on the wrong track. With God and your children on your side, who cares what THEY think. Yes, it hurts when you discover a child is not the least bit interested in something you have always wanted to do. Yes, it takes a certain amount of courage to defend them from well-meaning teachers and relatives who know just what they should do and how they should behave. No, it isn't easy to allow children to learn some things the hard way. But children need to be allowed to make some of their own rules and to learn to take the responsibility for those rules. Pray for the ability to love them when it is hard; for sensitivity and understanding when they are rude; and for a broad sense of humor to see through their quirks and bad times. Pray for the ability to stand by patiently while they pick themselves up when they fall down. And pray for the wisdom to laugh with them, not at them.

#7 "Humbly ask Him to remove our shortcomings."

No parents are ever going to be satisfied with the job they have done as parents. Most will worry and wonder about things they might have done differently.

One shortcoming that all parents have is the ability to blame themselves for everything that goes wrong in their children's lives or to suffer deep pangs of guilt if they do something wrong or against the law. Other parental shortcomings that are in abundance are being quick to judge or being too anxious to please, too short of temper, or downright rude. Parents can be guilty of belittling and badgering, of making dire predictions about children's future behavior, and of spending useless hours worrying over things that could happen but probably never will.

When doing Step Seven, ask yourself again if you might still be subtly asking your children to take sides against the alcoholic. Do you still harbor strong feelings against the alcoholic spouse for his treatment of the children? Are you expecting the children somehow to make up to you for the treatment you have received? The nondrinking parent in an alcoholic home is often on the defensive with everyone, including the children. Do you find yourself trying to defend your actions or attitudes to the rest of the family, and are you ever strongly on the defensive when there is no reason to be?

Parents can often be overheard teasing or ridiculing children for things they can not help (big nose, big ears), or they will laugh at something they choose to wear or do, make fun of their friends, or remind them of humiliating mistakes. These tactics seldom accomplish anything more than to make a child feel guilty and stupid.

God can help in the elimination of these parental shortcomings. He can support you in your genuine desire to give up being overly sensitive or cruel, and he can grant you the ability and the opportunity to learn new behaviors.

#8 "Made a list of all persons we had harmed and became willing to make amends to them all."

Taken in context of this booklet, Step Eight means making a list of past actions and omissions where your children are concerned.

Perhaps you have been overburdened with responsibilities and have not allowed enough time to talk and listen to them. If so, find a way to set aside some of your time for each individual child. The easiest way to do this is to take one child at a time for a walk, a ride, a shopping trip, out for a sandwich, or just to make yourself available at the kitchen table for a chat.

Have you realized how important it is to your children for you to show up at that school play, that important game, or some other function? Do you send them to church or take them? Resolve to make the effort to support them in all their activities just by being present when you can. On occasions when it is absolutely impossible for you to attend, draft a friend or relative to represent you. Afterwards, ask your child to repeat word for word, experience by experience what you were unable to attend or see for yourself.

Maybe you have been threatened by seeing your children develop relationships with other children or adults and have behaved badly out of petty jealousy. It is very important for children to get to know and love others outside the family. You can encourage this and be comforted by the knowledge that children's first allegiance is always to the parents even if they do not show it. Children, like animals, can become discouraged and act out if chained close.

As a parent, do you recognize the importance and desirability of teaching your children to maintain love and loyalty toward each other? Brothers and sisters need to be discouraged from petty infighting and competition for love. If they can be assured there is enough love and time available for everyone, they will develop a compassionate "one for all, all for one" attitude toward basic family unity.

If your list includes some really serious, harmful things, such as childbeating or bitter destruction of egos, the best way for you to make amends would be to seek professional counseling for both yourself and your child — from SOMEONE WHO UNDERSTANDS ALCOHOLISM.

#9 "Made direct amends to such people wherever possible except when to do so would injure them or others."

With Step Nine, you can begin to put into practice little things that you have learned make your children feel more important. Sometimes you may feel that you already gave so much to your children, you have nothing left for yourself. There are ways of making children feel good and important without losing all contact with yourself.

Within reason, allow your children freedom to pick out how they will spend their own free time. Give your children a small amount of money and teach them to buy you gifts for special occasions (Who is going to teach them to be thoughtful of you, if you don't?). Let them plan and prepare a meal while you take a bath or catch up on your reading. Allow children to do their own laundry (It will get better as time goes on). Have them take care of their own rooms in their own way (just shutting the door if nothing else). Encourage them to plan surprises for each other. Children need to know their opinions count in such things as what to have for dinner and what movie the family should see, so let them make choices whenever possible. This is not to say that you as a parent should not exercise good judgment when needed.

Give your children lots and lots of love and listen, listen, listen. Many times a parent thinks that if children bring a problem, they are expecting the parent to solve it. This is not always true. Sometimes children want to use a parent as a sounding board. At such times, they neither want you nor expect you to solve the problem or offer advice. Pass up the temptation to make yourself look important and all-knowing. Ask children directly which it is they want from you. If it is to solve the problem, ask yourself whether it would be wiser for you to do so or be better to help them explore possibilities and alternatives, leaving the final solution up to them. Once your children have decided on a course of action, resist any urge to say: "I told you so" if the action does not turn out well. The lesson they learn and your quiet supportiveness will make the biggest impression on them.

#10 "Continued to take personal inventory and when we were wrong promptly admitted it."

Many times a careless word, a thoughtless action, or even a deliberate decision can turn out to be detrimental to children's self-esteem or physical well-being. When that has happened, you can freely admit to children that you were remiss or made a mistake, without fear of losing face. If your children are over four years of age, they already know you are not perfect, and your admission of being human and capable of mistakes will only increase their respect for you. You will also set an example that will allow them to admit to making mistakes. If you are used to accepting children's apologies without recrimination, they will do the same for you.

#11 "Sought through prayer and meditation to improve our conscious contact with God as we understood Him, praying only for knoweldge of His will for us and the power to carry that out."

Parents of children of any age have times of intense frustration, times of great joy, and all the feelings in between. In talking over these times with your Higher Power, you can ask for guidance, give heartfelt thanks, pray for knowledge to do God's will, and ask God to help you stop gritting your teeth. Whatever your needs are, you can rest assured that they are known and will be answered according to his will. Praying only for His will can quiet your anxieties and give you peace and comfort.

It is very difficult, at first, to pray *only* for God's will without slipping in a little something about how you would like things to be, particularly if a child is ill or in trouble. It is comforting if you realize that God Himself was a parent and understands your deepest needs and sorrows.

#12 "Having had a spiritual awakening as the result of these steps, we tried to carry this message to others and to practice these principles in all our affairs."

By the time you reach Step Twelve, you will discover that you are a much calmer and more confident parent. By then you will probably also notice some constructive changes in your children's behavior and attitudes. You and your children are involved in a growth process that aims to help each find his own identity and that focuses on family closeness rather than on the hurt and pain of past days. Each of you can recognize your own needs unashamedly and make room for those needs in the total family workings.

Your children will have been exposed to love, sharing, and forgiveness and they will carry these messages to their peer groups. You can use what you have learned from your experiences to help other troubled parents learn to cope with the special problems that occur in families where one parent is an alcoholic.

Putting the Twelve Steps into practice takes diligence, much desire, and the involvement of the nondrinking parent and each child in the family. You will discover the effort to be worthwhile, as you see your children bloom and grow. You will discover yourself to have a more relaxed and confident attitude, and you will find the joy that exists in family understanding and unity — whether or not the alcoholic in the family stops drinking.

The coping techniques described above are not meant to take the place of professional counseling, if that is needed, nor will they always be effective in dealing with the more troubled child. As a parent, you must take into consideration the losses suffered by every single member in an alcoholic family, the special problems that may arise for children who have been physically abused, the important distinction between neglect and detachment, and the difficulty in switching the focus from the alcoholic's behavior to the behavior of the family as a whole. It is important to get the best help available for your child and to do so is not an admission of failure, but rather, an indication of love and caring.

Alateen and Alatot can go a long way in helping your children understand the illness of alcoholism. Your support and understanding at home can go a long way in helping children to understand themselves. Through the teachings of the Al-Anon programs, you and your children will learn that your lives need not center around the alcoholic's ups and downs, but around your own needs and the desires of the family as a whole unit.

It must be emphasized here that you and your children are not in any way forming an alliance against the alcoholic. You are learning survival in a difficult and personally threatening situation, and you are forming new, honest, open-communication relationships with each other in the family. If the drinking parent is still drinking and living in the home, he may see this new behavior and new relationship as a threat; he might make attempts to thwart it. Your Al-Anon groups will help you contend with this. As your strength and detachment skills develop, you will know what to do.

One distinct problem the nondrinking parent always faces is how to cope with the drinking parent who continues to manipulate the children: the conning, the broken promises, the punishment, the accusations against the nondrinking parent, the contradictions. You might be able to ignore these matters as they affect you alone; it is very difficult and sometimes impossible to be a bystander while these things are taking place and involving the children. You know you will be left to pick up the pieces. However, it is much easier to maintain a balanced and calm attitude if you realize that there is only so much you can do in the way of protecting the children. If you teach them about the illness of alcoholism, help them to learn detachment skills, give them a sense of their own worth and identity, and prevent them from being physically abused, then you will have given them the necessary tools to be self-reliant while being compassionate toward the alcoholic parent. Once they have learned to cope with the illness of alcoholism, what in life won't they be able to handle?

Postscript

In the final analysis, once you as a parent have recognized the special needs of a child and have done everything you can to provide for those needs, it is well to remember the Al-Anon admonition: LET GO AND LET GOD.

God, thank you for this child of mine.
Please make for him the sun to shine.
Help me to give love and caring
Without smothering or ensnaring.
Help me set examples too
That show my love and faith in you.
Give me the strength to meet his needs
And the ability to forgive misdeeds.
Help me to be wise and kind
And instill good things into his mind.
Give me insight that I may hear
When he is crying out in fear.
Please grant me humor that I may smile
When I must walk that extra mile,
And Lord, please help me find in you
The strength and patience to carry through
With this precious burden you've given me,
Always putting my faith in Thee.